SHADOWS & LUMINESCENCE

Vadim Chervin

Shadows & Luminescence

Published by Spines
ISBN: 979-8-89383-513-7

SHADOWS & LUMINESCENCE

VADIM CHERVIN

CHAPTER I
SHADOWS & LUMINESCENCE

Beneath the veil of twilight's blush,

Where whispers float in the poetic hush,

There lies a realm, both vast and deep,

Where secrets of the heart do sleep.

In every shadow, every gleam,

Lies a story, of a silent dream.

A tapestry of time unspun,

Beneath the gaze of the setting sun.

Words unspoken, tales untold,

In the heart, they quietly mold.

A silent dance of light and shade,

In the spaces where a bright light fades.

Yet, from the quiet depths arise,

Verses that soar into the skies.

Each line, a brushstroke on the night,

Painting the dark with words of light.

A poem, a whisper in the breeze,

A melody amongst the trees.

A beacon for the weary soul,

Guiding them towards their final goal.

So let the words flow, pure and true,

From the depths of me and on to you.

A bridge across the silent space,

A tender, timeless, ethereal grace.

CHAPTER 2
A BLINK
MOMENT IN TIME

In the gentle embrace of dawn's first light,

I stir from slumber's deep embrace,

As morning's hues paint the sky so bright,

And the world awakens with grace.

With drowsy eyes, I greet the day,

Each blink is a moment of sweet transition,

A dance of light in a tranquil way,

In the quiet stillness of dawn's rendition.

The morning dew, like nature's tears,

Glistens upon the earth's green canvas,

Whispering secrets to attentive ears,

In a symphony of silence, so vast.

With each flutter of my eyelids' flight,

The world around me subtly rearranges,

A kaleidoscope of fleeting sights,

In a dance of ever-changing exchanges.

Oh, how my soul sings with the sunrise,

As I surrender to the day's tender embrace,

In this timeless dance, where moments arise,

And each blink reveals a new, wondrous space.

CHAPTER 3
A BRAND-NEW LOVE

In the realm of love, so vast and wide,

Not every soul shall have a bride.

Yet each may find, in life's grand play,

One heart that doth not stray away.

Seize thou must, with fervent grip,

Lest love, like sand, through fingers slip.

Cherish it as the summer's day,

For upheld, it fades away.

When at last love's light is seen,

Regret will mark what might have been.

For thou hast missed the gate ajar,

Now sealed, its key flung far.

Thus, hold love tight, when it doth appear,

In its warmth, let thy heart cheer.

For lost chances ring a somber tone,

A heart once open, now turned to stone.

CHAPTER 4
A MOUNTAIN DWELLING

Amidst the mist, a contradiction stands,

No walls to guard, yet a fortress grand,

Like drawing water from stone's embrace,

A citadel poised at nature's grace.

An ancient edifice, a timeless sight,

Eclipsing aspirations, beyond our might,

Enshrined in solitude, in the mountain's hold,

A bastion of strength, a story untold.

At its zenith, a beacon's blaze,

A signal of power, through nights and days,

Defying challenges with a steadfast cry,

Invincible, under the vast sky.

A testament to resolve, for all to heed,

A declaration of sovereignty, indeed,

Above the fray of mortal desire,

A fortress beyond man's reach or fire.

For a millennium, it stands tall,

Quieting fears with its towering thrall,

Above the clouds, in a tranquil embrace,

Rulers of destiny, in their sovereign grace.

CHAPTER 5
A PIECE OF MIND

A piece of mind

Is picking from behind

A value of words that I may want to say

That may come out later in the day

Division from subterranean internal

Considering exceptions of external

Within the realm of social accepting

Not to impress on physical connecting

Tornado of thought confusion

To keep up with existing external illusion

To maintain the visual perception

Of my personality public exception

Keeping up the makeup of my face

To maintain validity and grace

Accommodating a variety of branding

For an acceptable society good standing

CHAPTER 6
A SET STAGE OF LOVE

Upon the stage of love, a scene unfolds,

Where hearts entwine in a dance divine,

the backdrop of stars, so bold,

Two souls converge in a rhythm, so fine.

The stage is set with passion's fire,

As lovers' gazes meet in an embrace,

Their passions ignite with burning desire,

As they surrender to love's sweet embrace.

With each whispered word and gentle touch,

They paint a portrait of devotion pure,

Their love, an epic tale, unfolding as such,

In every gesture, every sigh, they ensure.

The stage of love, a sacred space,

Where dreams take flight and hearts unite,

In a timeless bond, they find their place,

And bask in the glow of love's eternal light.

CHAPTER 7
A THOUGHT OF CAUTION

Foreseen and yet not avoided still

My mind is my forever and never ending teacher

A pounding never stopping at my will

Commending me like a Sunday preacher

Protecting from uncommon situations

A jolt to stop and simply look around

Make necessary evaluations and preparations

Then with certainty to stay solid on my ground

Consensus of what is and what was

Scanning the memories for any resolution

Blank stare confined in a momentary pause

Awaiting a commitment to a solution

Like looking through an old dusty attic

Surprised by long forgotten things of the past

Searching with the dedication of a fanatic

As if preparing for a final test

CHAPTER 8
A THOUGHT THAT GOT CAUGHT

Inspiring the stimulus of joyful intention

Pulling the strings of ideas passing without reflection

Playing them like a heavenly harp

To a tune of spontaneous perfection

The emptiness is being filled like a pool

Taking the shape of the set-in borders

Infiltration of the senses tool

Stimulating a new set of orders

A constant highway of variational thought

Zipping by, without notice

Unknown to one who keeps track

In the appendix of the mind, one is finally got caught

CHAPTER 9
A TOUCH

In the soft light of dawn, as morning breaks,

I reach out, drawn by the love that awakes.

Your presence beside me, a comforting sight,

Fills my heart with warmth, like morning's light.

As my hand finds yours, a gentle touch,

I'm reminded of the depth of our love's clutch.

The smoothness of your skin beneath my palm,

Eases my worries, like a calming balm.

In that fleeting moment, as our fingers intertwine,

I feel a connection, divine and sublime.

For in your touch, I find solace and peace,

A sanctuary where all troubles cease.

So, I linger in that moment, in the quiet embrace,

Grateful for the love that time cannot erase.

With your hand in mine, I feel whole and complete,

In this precious moment, our love bond is replete.

CHAPTER 10
A VISION COME TO LIFE

I move through thoughts of inspiration
Like bird sores through an open sky
Through muses sizzling veins pulsation
My cause to feel like I can fly

My words, cascading waterfall
Foaming together, pushing, pressing
Transmitted here for one and all
In the grasp of innovative blessing

Within the void of wanting, feeling
Untapped potential opens a page
And words start piling on the ceiling
A poem is born, a brand new stage

No holding back the glow is there

The pen is scribbling transmission

Through muse penetrating stare

Manifestation of a vision

CHAPTER 11
ANCIENT FORT

A contradiction of a sort

No walls in sight, but still a fort

Like squeezing water from the stone

Upon waterfall glimmering at dawn

An ancient structure seen by all

Unreachable by any goal

Secure in all surrounding direction

On mountain peak to prevent insurrection

A fire at the top burns bright

Seen from afar to state it's might

Challenging all, don't even try

Unconquerable, without question why

Built as a statement for enemies to know

We shall not be concord, so just go

On top of the world of human desire

Fort can't be reached by man or fire

Standing strong for a thousand years

Putting to rest its inhabitance so many fears

Above the clouds, all are very safe

Ruling supreme are strong and brave!

CHAPTER 12
ANOTHER DAY HAS DAWNED

Another day has dawned another vision

Another door set free a new poetic composition

The corridors inside my head are echoing with tremor

Resonating like a bell from this freed endeavor

My fingers are in full tension like a trigger

Ready to write words down and configure

Ready to lay down poetic lines in rapid fire

For this world to intake and admire

I am the pen in the hands of a higher power

Laying down words to build another tower

The engineer of absolution and redemption

In the unending metropolis of visional perception

Soaring above it like a bird caught in a stream

Of creativities untethered verbal dream

Without judgment or discrimination of this spark

I am just a beam of light releasing poems from the dark

CHAPTER 13
APPROACHING WORDS

In the vast expanse of thought's terrain,

My mind races, seeking to attain

The perfect words to bring to light,

Ideas that dance in shadows, out of sight.

Like swans gliding on a tranquil lake,

My thoughts traverse, each one awake.

Emotions stir, a fiery stake,

Igniting passions, no room for mistake.

Yet beliefs stand firm, a wall of resistance,

Challenging choices, testing persistence.

Words struggle to find their existence,

Amidst the chaos, in their persistence.

But through the turmoil, a path is found,

Words emerge from the depths, unbound.

Each one chosen, each one crowned,

In the symphony of thought, they resound.

CHAPTER 14
AS ANOTHER SUNRISE

As another sunrise graces the stage,

With hues of orange and pink engage,

The night's curtain gently draws away,

Revealing shadows in the light's sway.

The sky paints itself in tones of blue,

A spectacle that's ever anew,

Each morning breath fills my chest,

As a new day begins its quest.

In the face of such grandeur,

I stand, Awaiting, embracing what's at hand,

Like unwrapping a gift, a delight,

Joy and happiness take flight.

Worries recede, troubles fade,

For now, they're left in the shade,

With a cup of coffee in my grasp,

A morning friend, to soothe and clasp.

CHAPTER 15
AS I AWAKE

When I awake in fear and doubt

I toss and turn in pain throughout

I think of God, and I reach out

And start to say these words out loud

O Lord, I thank you for my health

For all the things that you have provided me

for all the happiness and wealth

And for your hand that's there to guide me

I thank you for my family

For joy, they feel because of me

And all the good you have done for me

For all the love I feel inside of me

I thank you for another day

That I can see the life surrounding me

For the improvements in my way

And for the light, you burn inside of me

And all the darkness fades away

My mind clears up from all the fear

And now I can begin my day

With mind and body free and clear

CHAPTER 16
AS BRIDGES OF THOUGHT

As bridges of thought, our minds entwine,

Whereon we meet, our hearts align.

In silent pact, our love declared,

In mental grasp, our souls are ensnared.

Hand in hand, though but a dream,

Our hearts conflate a seamless stream.

Melodies of love, our souls' sweet song,

In harmony, where we belong.

Through mirrored gaze, we see our truth,

In unity, our endless youth.

As summer's breeze, so soft, so light,

Our spirits dance, pure and bright.

No need for words, our hearts converse,

In love's own language, deep and terse.

Like rivers rush from heights so tall,

Our connection flows, encompassing all.

In this moment, profound and sweet,

Soulmates found, in silence meet.

A bond so deep, a love so pure,

Eternal, steadfast, ever sure.

As our mental connection builds bridges

That we used to meet and declare our love for each other

As I hold your hand in a mental state

Our hearts melt together

And our souls intoned into a melody of love

We see each other through one another's eyes, we know each other as ourselves

We feel each other as if a cool breath on a hot summer day

No words are necessary as our love flows through us like a river cascading from a waterfall

And that is the moment of true connection of soul mate's

CHAPTER 17
AS YOU HOLD ME IN THE NIGHT

As you hold me in the night's embrace,

I feel the warmth of your tender grace.

Your arms around me, strong and tight,

Shield me from the darkness of the night.

In your embrace, I find my solace,

In your touch, I feel the promise

Of safety, love, and endless care,

Wrapped in the comfort of being there.

With every beat of your steady heart,

I found a haven, a brand-new start.

The worries of the day drift away,

In the sanctuary where we both lay.

As you hold me, the world stands still,

And in your arms, I feel the thrill

Of knowing that I'm truly loved,

In your embrace, forever moved.

So, hold me close, throughout the night,

In your arms, everything feels right.

For as you hold me, love's pure light,

Guides us through till morning's sight.

CHAPTER 18
CAVE

In the heart of the mountain's deep embrace,

Where shadows dance in the cavern's grace,

The Wanderers tread with courage bold,

Through labyrinths of stone, their tale unfolds.

A maze within a maze, they roam,

Seeking an exit, an escape, a home,

Yet every turn, every twist, they find,

Leads them back to where they've been confined.

But still, they press, undeterred by despair,

For hope burns bright, a beacon rare,

With each step taken, they defy the dark,

And strive to find the light, to make their mark.

Through tunnels winding, ever long,

Their voices rise in a hopeful song,

For though the path ahead may be unclear,

They journey on, undaunted by fear.

With every sunrise, a new chance is born,

To unravel the mysteries, to weather the storm,

And so, they rest, with dreams of tomorrow,

For in the heart of the mountain, lies hope to borrow.

CHAPTER 19
CELEBRATE YOUR FEATS

Celebrate your feats, the triumphs you've spun,

Bask in the glow of victories won.

Enveloped in warmth from those you hold dear,

Let melodies surround, bringing cheer near.

Ease your hold, let serenity bloom,

Release your burdens, dispel the gloom.

Feel the earth 'neath soles lightly tread,

In silent mirth, your spirit's fed.

As if soaring in a nocturnal flight,

Where dreams lift you into the night.

Every desire within your grasp,

Life unfolds gently, in joy you clasp.

Floating on dreams, where all is light,

Every hope within sight is so bright.

Life's river glides, serene and rich,

A seamless journey, without a hitch.

CHAPTER 20
CLAIM YOUR WORLD

Claim your world, let the secrets unfold,

Craft your reality, brave and bold.

With every step, take charge of your fate,

Turn dreams into action, it's never too late.

The power's yours to shape each day and night,

In every challenge, find your might.

Your life's canvas awaits your vibrant hue,

The masterpiece of the world that's truly you.

Let not fear or doubt cloud your sky,

Stand tall, reach far, and aim high.

You are the captain of your soul's voyage,

Turning each page to your advantage.

Embrace your power, let your spirit soar,

Unlock the potential you hold in store.

With vision clear and heart steadfast,

Make your present bright, and your future vast.

So, possess your world, let your light shine through,

In every moment, be bold, be true.

Forge your path with the strength within,

And watch the magic of your life begin.

CHAPTER 21
CRAVE

Crave, a whisper in the silent night,

A longing born from depths so tight.

It pulls at heartstrings, deep and true,

Urging us to pursue what's due.

It's the hunger that, stirs within,

A restless urge beneath the skin.

To seek, to strive, to reach so high,

Crave drives us forward, to touch the sky.

It fuels the fire, ignites the soul,

Pushing us towards our ultimate goal.

With every breath, with every beat,

Craving propels us to stand on our feet.

But heed its call with careful heed,

For craving can sow both want and need.

Balance its pull with wisdom's guide,

And let it be your ally, not your pride.

So, embrace the craving that stirs within,

Let it fuel your journey to begin.

With passion as your guiding light,

You'll conquer mountains, and reach new heights.

CHAPTER 22
CRUMBLING HEART

As your heart breaks, tears blur your sight,

Clear lipstick on lips, a silent plea for one more night,

His shoulder, your hair, entwined in a final embrace,

A bittersweet moment, time slowing its pace.

Friends turned lovers, intertwined souls,

His touch, his warmth, made you feel whole,

Undercovers, in whispers, secrets shared,

Now he's leaving, and you're left bare.

Staring at his retreating figure, aching inside,

Every fiber of your being screaming, "Don't hide!",

You want to run, to beg him to stay,

But all you feel is your heart's disarray.

You know she doesn't love him like you do,

That false happiness she offers won't be true,

Yet he walks away, blind to your plea,

Leaving behind a shattered you, a broken plea.

The little girl within you weeps, her cries so loud,

While the outer shell crumbles, lost in the crowd,

His fading steps echo in your ears,

Sealing the door on your love, on your fears.

You're left wandering, lost and torn,

No solace found in the coming morn,

Your mind is a whirlwind of regret and pain,

Longing for a chance to start again.

But he's gone, and you're left to mourn,

In the shadows of love, now forlorn,

Your heart shattered, your soul adrift,

As you search for a way to heal, to lift.

In the silence, in the emptiness, you tread,

Haunted by memories of what's now dead,

But deep within, a flicker of hope remains,

That one day, you'll break free from these chains.

CHAPTER 23
DANCING FLOOR

The music deafening my senses

As the body drops all the fences

The beat is pulsating through my heart

The hips are starting at their part

The head is following the beat

The brow is sweating with the heat

Shoulders are joining the twist

The motion is moving to the wrist

The beat is taking over, storming

The dance type movement slowly forming

And before you realize

The music is glowing in your eyes

You quickly get into rhythms spell
Using the moves you know so well
And then before you know
You're now in the familiar flow

Your arms are doing scissors in the air
Twisting hips as much as you would dare
The feet are moving on their own
Ready to dance into the dawn

You're dancing like the floor beneath you
Is moving and vibrating with you
The crowd is moving like a wave
To satisfy the dancing crave

CHAPTER 24
DON'T BE AFRAID OF CHANGE!

Change, a paradoxical companion,

A road sign on the lazy ego's terrain,

For some, a mere fork in the path,

For others, a peak above the clouds, untamed.

Fear grips us in the face of the unseen,

Clutching to the comfort of the known,

Reluctant to venture beyond the familiar scene,

Yet change beckons, a new journey to be shown.

Change, the steadfast force shaping our world,

A golden thread waiting to be found,

Once embraced, like a breath of cold,

An "ahh" of clarity, without a single doubt.

I welcome you, Change, with arms wide open,

Eager to be amazed, to be shown,

Wrap me in your enigmatic embrace,

For I'll walk with you into the great unknown.

Change, you hold within your endless possibilities,

A canvas awaiting the strokes of fate,

Though uncertainties may cloud our vision,

Together, we'll navigate, we'll create.

With each step into the new, the unfamiliar,

I'll embrace the challenges, the charms you bear,

For in the dance of change, in the flow of time,

I'll discover new horizons and new joys to share.

CHAPTER 25
DREAM STALLIONS

As I lay down on my pillow, resting

My eyelids are my theater curtain

Shapes in the dark, start arranging, forming, casting

Above another world, all is uncertain!

All of a sudden, I'm in a fairytale like slay

Of blue and gold floating above the ground

Four horses pulling the slay, each in a different way

My heart beats still, and there's no sound!

A stallion of white, gray brown, and black

Each one as beautiful and wild as the rest

Soaring above a startling, stage deck

White stallion starts getting higher fast

Dream stallions where do you make me go

Where are you pulling my imagination

what waits ahead for me, I just don't know

What will you drag me through, what situation

I find myself in a field of never ending green

with children's laughter all around me

A little girl screams out Irene

I'm going to hide so come and find me

I feel so peaceful and so calm

The sun is warm like a cozy cover

And as I open up my palm

A small gray scallion I uncover

I set him on the grassy ground

And ask him, what is coming next

He looked at me and then turned around

And off we go without a text

We travel over great lakes glaze

Up on it, I can see a reflection

As I try taking a closer gaze

My mind is making some connection

I see my family, my friends

Our trip to barbecue and fishing

A look at the familiar trends

And all the things that I have been wishing

We start to rise into the sky

As I looked up the stallion changed

A brown stallion is now my ride,

the world again is rearranged

From such great heights, I barely see

My life's familiar surrounding

I call the ones that dear to me

But they are not responding

But as the skies darken, a chill fills the air,

A black stallion leads, with an ominous stare,

Descending into darkness, fear grips my soul,

Lost in a realm where shadows take their toll.

I really don't want to dwell here

The darkest corner of my mind

This place is stressful and constant fear

And there's no way out that I can find

Yet each night, before I drift away to sleep,

I call upon the white stallion, my dreams to keep,

For in its guidance, I find solace and light,

Navigating through the depths of night.

Dream stallions, visiting with tales untold,

Each night, a new adventure to behold,

Contrasting sights within my mind's domain,

What visions haunt you, within your dreams reign?

CHAPTER 26
EMOTIONAL SPLATTER

In the swirling tempest of emotions set free,

Splattering across the canvas of my inner sea,

Emotional compost, a tangled mess,

As damp fog chokes, blinding distress.

Dark clouds loom, obscuring the sun's glow,

Casting shadows on the beauty below,

A stillness descends, a cold embrace,

Heavy-heartedness etched on my face.

I bury my face in the pillow's soft embrace,

Hoping for change, a new visual grace,

But alas, the heaviness remains,

An awakening, scourged by unseen chains.

The weight of the world, a burden to bear,

As I stumble through the fog, unaware,

Yearning for clarity, for light to shine,

In this adversarial realm, where darkness entwines.

Yet amidst the turmoil, a glimmer of hope,

A flicker of resilience, a way to cope,

For in the depths of despair, there lies strength,

To rise above, to go the length.

So, I face the day, though heavy it may be,

With courage and resolve, I'll finally break free,

From the grip of concern, from the fog's embrace,

Towards dawn, towards a brighter space.

CHAPTER 27
EXERCISE

Exercise, the cornerstone of health,

Our body, our temple, in its wealth,

A vessel for the soul's journey's toll,

Physical fitness, is our ultimate goal.

To sculpt our body, to fortify,

Its outer walls, beneath the sky,

A flat stomach, a back erect,

A posture tall, without defect.

To carve the chest, a perfect form,

Muscles like steel, resilient and warm,

Time invested, no room for debate,

With determination, we elevate.

From ancient times to modern day,

Exercise guides us on our way,

Referenced in texts of old,

Practice valued; a tale retold.

From Greek philosophers' insight,

To modern science's guiding light,

Exercise remains, a timeless art,

Nurturing body, mind, and heart.

CHAPTER 28
FAME

Fame, a fleeting flame that lights the sky,

Bringing adoration, but also a sigh.

It shines so bright, yet burns so fast,

Leaving behind a shadow of the past.

Some chase its glow with relentless zeal,

Believing it holds the power to heal.

But fame, like a fickle friend, may deceive,

Leaving those who seek it to some grieve.

For fame's allure is but a transient gleam,

A shimmering illusion, not what it seems.

It blinds the eyes to life's true treasures,

Leading hearts astray with false measures.

True worth lies not in fame's fleeting grasp,

But in the depth of one's soul, a steadfast clasp.

In kindness shown and deeds done well,

In love shared and stories to tell.

So let not the quest for fame consume,

For its rewards may lead to a lonely gloom.

Instead, seek the path of purpose and light,

And let your legacy shine, pure and bright.

CHAPTER 29
FINDING DIRECTION

Walking through the essence of the day

Step after step, slowly choosing a direction

Moving so mindful in a particular sway

Without concern for utter perfection

Sidewalk, like a red carpet in front of me rolled out

Grass on the sides like strolling, guiding lights

As if the road without any doubt

Is corresponding to my undetermined sights

Leading my subconscious into the new

And step by step I am getting closer yet

Without paying attention or a spew

Exactly to where I am supposed to get!

THIS WAY
THAT WAY

CHAPTER 30
FOR EVERY SOUL

For every soul beneath the sun,

I wish your dreams would be overrun

By visions true to only you,

Not swayed by crowds or fleeting views.

Opinions vast as stars in the skies,

Yet in your heart, the truth lies.

May life be kind, your journey light,

Blessed with love that shines so bright.

May joy be found in the work you do,

With life's sweet gifts bestowed on you.

May smiles grace your days, come what may,

Striding forth in your own unique way.

Eyes on the prize, let nothing sway

Your path, as it unfolds your way.

The steps, once blurred, now shine so clear,

Drawing every cherished dream near.

In this tapestry of hopes and dreams,

Where every stitch is more than it seems,

I wish for you to find your place,

And walk your journey with grace and pace.

CHAPTER 31
GAME OF KINGS

Opposing armies, willingness expressed

Met on the field of the mixed terrain

To do the things that they do best

It matters not under the sun or rain

Moving around in practiced moves for sure

Upon the field of their choice and liking

Make sure each one of them secure

Before the next line started striking

Make sure the others won't start guessing

With soldiers, horses, moves are ready

To where the main line is pressing

The knights are moving from behind them steady

Soldiers are moving slow then stay

Putting some holes in their defense

To give the knights and horses way

Protecting the queen in her offense

And after all is said and done

With towers might under the protection

Opposing king now starts to run

Trying to escape from all this action

Opposing troops are being seized

Dark King is cornered in his gate

The white king now is very pleased

With battle's end and dark king fate

The dark king fell, new one will reign

It's all about, whose army lasts

As the new game will begin again

It's a game of kings, it's a game of chess

CHAPTER 32
GYPSY DANCER

Upon the darkness of a dream

A vision starting to come through

Like a movie starting on the screen

A seen becoming clear and true

A skirt of red with black I see

The shoes beneath with velvet sway

Lifting skirt crease, revealing a knee

By gentle hands in a stylish way

As seen is moving slowly up

And the skirt starts to become a dress

Thin waist, corset style on the top

A gentle arm holds crease in stress

Shoulders revealed, standing the guard

Bared, beautiful, and strong

Awaiting, ready for a start

A dance to now a faded song

To match the dress a rose in hand

With elbow raffles hanging in a statement

In a familiar for her stand

Begins the movement of enchantment

Behind the wavy hair of raven black

On background of the strings of a guitar

Revealing a pointy chin and long thin neck

As the faded voice of the song comes from afar

With every step, sway, every glance,

A gypsy dancer lost in her art,

She weaves a spell, as if in a trance,

Capturing the essence of her wild heart.

A gypsy song like chant gets louder still

Her twisting body moving hands in grace

In turn, her hair is moving back at will

I finally can see her lovely face

CHAPTER 33
HEAT

A scorching unforgiving heat

Like fog sets over the sweating ground

Covering me from the head down to my feet

Exerting me without a sound

A haze that clings, throthe ugh skin it seers.

It cloaks me whole, an unwelcome sheath,

In swelter's grip, relentless, fierce,

In silence deep, it steals my breath.

To wrapped in its essence hard to even move

Sucking on my energy like a thirsty vampire

It's not for me I think need a different groove

As more and more I lay here and slowly tire

I'm trying to cool down in water vapor

Conniving heat keeps grasping at it first it its escaped me without any savor

I just wish to be cool and quench my thirst

CHAPTER 34
HER EVENING SKY

In the evening's embrace, cool and serene,

As the sunset's light begins to fade unseen,

A table set, exquisite in its design,

Under a canopy of stars, our love is defined.

You glow softly in the dimming light,

The heater's flame whispers secrets in the night,

I gaze at you, a vision so divine,

A treasure to hold, forever mine.

Hold her close, the dearest part of your soul,

Cherish her with every breath, every role,

Never let her know a moment of despair,

With laughter and love, handle her with care.

Offer her your strength, your comforting embrace,

Wrap her in love, in every possible space,

Be her shelter in life's tempestuous rise,

And in every storm, be her blue skies

CHAPTER 35
HUNS HELMET

In the silence of history's shadowed hall,

Stands the helmet of the Hun, noble and tall.

Forged in the fires of olden times,

Adorned with feathers, the warrior's chimes.

Turquoise inlays on darkened steel,

Coral and gold, the power they seal.

Wings of the eagle, the fur of the beast,

From eastern steppes to the royal feast.

Cheek guards embossed with tales of war,

Nose guard stands for the battle's bore.

A crest of fur, status unspoken,

Feathers like words, promises unbroken.

Upon deep blue, it fiercely shines,

An echo of the past, in present times.

This helm, a symphony of ancient might,

Bears the essence of Hunnic fight.

In every etching, the sagas we find,

Of warriors fierce, of a regal kind.

The silent music of a bygone age,

Now immortalized on history's page.

CHAPTER 36
I AM GRATEFUL

In moments still, I take a breath,

Grateful for life, for love, for death.

For every dawn and twilight hue,

For skies of gray and skies of blue.

I'm grateful for the morning sun,

Its golden rays, a new day began.

For gentle rains that kiss the ground,

And rainbow hues that dance around.

Grateful for the air I breathe,

For whispered winds through every leaf.

For songs of birds that fill the air,

Their melodies are beyond compare.

I'm grateful for the gift of sight,

To see the stars that shine at night.

For hands to touch and hold so dear,

For every smile that brings me cheer.

Grateful for each step I take,

For every choice, for every mistake.

For lessons learned along the way,

That shaped me into who I am today.

In gratitude, my heart finds peace,

For life's wonders, big and petite.

I bow my head, I close my eyes,

And offer thanks beneath the skies.

CHAPTER 37
I HEAR YOU IN YOUR SLEEP

In the quiet of the night's embrace,

When stars twinkle with gentle grace,

I hear you in your tranquil sleep,

In whispers soft, in dreams so deep.

Your breath, a rhythm, calm and light,

Guides me through the darkest night.

With every sigh, a lullaby,

A melody that fills the sky.

I hear you in your peaceful rest,

A gentle breeze upon my chest.

Your slumber's song, a soothing sound,

In sleep, a treasure is truly found.

Though worlds may spin, and troubles keep,

In dreams, your presence, pure and deep.

I listen closely, and in the night,

I hear you in your whispered flight.

So, sleep, my dear, and dream away,

In realms where worries fade and sway.

For in your sleep, I find my peace,

And in your dreams, my heart's release.

CHAPTER 38
IDEAS TAKE WING

Within the realm where thoughts are born and brewed,

In pools of knowledge, old and oft reviewed,

Through mental mazes, inspiration threads,

In comfort zones of yet unproven creds.

It strikes, a wave's crest in a moment's grace,

Splashing visions clear upon your face.

And as the tide recedes, it leaves behind

A spark, an "Aha!" moment unconfined.

Like meteors that streak the velvet night,

Ideas blaze, born from the mental fight.

Not judged as wrong or right in their first flight,

They dart across the mind's sky, burning bright.

In this poetic space where dreams are spun,

Each thought, a star, a galaxy began.

From deep within, where creativity lies,

Ideas take wing, bound for uncharted skies.

CHAPTER 39
IN A WHIRLWIND OF THOUGHTS

In a whirlwind of thoughts, too dense and rich,

I find myself caught, a mental stitch.

Worries cling like shadows, long and dark,

One task at hand, yet miles off the mark.

Why do these concerns, unbidden, stay?

Is it my fault they haunt me night and day?

Damaged or insecure, I query,

Seeking the cure, a path less dreary.

A remedy sought, for peace, for light,

To ease the tumult of endless night.

I loathe this feeling, this restless deal,

Craving change, a new wheel to wheel.

I yearn for peace, a soothing breeze,
To change hearts and minds with ease.
A shoulder to lean on, support to find,
To stay the course, peace of mind.

To grasp my life's true essence, clearly,
Touch lives to foster cheer.
To be the dream I dare to dream,
Silencing the internal scream.

To scale heights unseen, vast and wide,
Greatness in my stride.
Firm on life's path, my fears uncast,
No shadows of doubt to be recast.

For every soul that breathes, I wish,
To chase their dreams, their bliss.
A dream I've harbored, deep and keen,
For hope and joy to reign, unseen.

CHAPTER 40
IN THE REALM OF SHADOWS

In a realm where shadows cast a doubt,

Where will is chained, and fears shout loud,

A soul is caught in a cage unseen,

Wrestling with what could have been.

Contained within air's silent walls,

Grasping at thoughts that endlessly call.

A journey through quicksand, heavy and dire,

Each step is an echo in a choir of mire.

Chains of thought, heavy, unseen,

Bind the spirit, keeping it keen.

Blood courses, a pressured stream,

Stress shapes the body, a relentless dream.

Each burdened step, a titan's weight,

Striving forward, tempting fate.

Yet in this dream where I strive to flee,

I stand immobile, longing to be free.

The chains within, of mightiest force,

Hold tighter still, without remorse.

Endless descent into dreams so tall,

Where fears whisper, "You might fall."

Yet within this struggle, a truth rings clear,

The strength to overcome, the will to steer.

For even as darkness tries to conceal,

The light of resolve, it cannot steal.

CHAPTER 41
IN THE DAYS OF PLAYGROUND LAUGHTER

In the days of playground laughter, so carefree,

We forged bonds without a second thought.

"Let's be friends!" - a phrase filled with glee,

Creating connections that time couldn't blot.

Those friendships, pure and unrefined,

Stood the test of time, resilient and true.

A treasure trove of memories intertwined,

Growing stronger with each passing view.

But as we age, barriers start to rise,

Trust becomes scarce, and hearts grow wary.

We shield ourselves from unseen guise,

And friendships dwindle, visions dreary.

Yet, amidst the haze of life's complexity,

We must reclaim the innocence of yore.

Open our hearts with joyful propensity,

And friendships will flourish once more.

So, let's recall those childhood days,

When making friends was effortless and pure.

With open arms and genuine ways,

We'll build connections that will endure.

CHAPTER 42
IN THE GENTLE CURVE OF YOUR SMILE

In the gentle curve of your smile, I find solace,
A sanctuary where my troubles are embraced,
Your eyes, pools of warmth and endless grace,
Reflecting love in every gaze.

Like the moonlight dancing on tranquil seas,
Your presence soothes my soul with ease,
Guiding me through life's tumultuous seas,
With you, my love, I find perfect peace.

In your touch, I feel the strength of mountains,
A steadfast anchor amidst life's fountains,
Your embrace, a fortress against the tides,
Where storms may rage, but love abides.

With every word you speak, a symphony I hear,

Melodies of love whispered in my ear,

You're the canvas upon which my dreams appear,

In your arms, I find home, forever near.

You're not just a queen in name, but indeed,

A ruler of hearts, with love as your creed,

In your presence, I find all that I need,

My eternal love, my queen indeed.

CHAPTER 43
IN THE LABYRINTH OF THOUGHT

In the labyrinth of thought, a random spark ignites,

A fleeting speculation, dancing in the night.

Emotions stir within, a battle to be fought,

As memories of lost ones, in the mind are caught.

Some depart unwillingly, torn from our embrace,

While others let go, choosing a different space.

Yet they linger on, like echoes in the wind,

Leaving behind a legacy, a story to rescind.

Moments etched in time, woven into our soul,

Each memory is a thread, shaping us as a whole.

Some evoke laughter, some bring tears,

But each one holds the essence of our yesteryears.

The love we shared, the arguments we'd make,

Over missteps taken, or the perfect cake.

These memories define us, like snowflakes unique,

An intricate mosaic, in the gallery of life we seek.

CHAPTER 44
IN THE LEDGER OF MY LIFE

In the ledger of my life, each year finds its place,

Stacked neatly on the shelf of time's embrace.

They bear witness to the journey I've trod,

The highs and lows, the paths I've plod.

The youth I squandered, a fleeting dream,

A cautionary tale in the grander scheme.

But I refuse to dwell on what's been lost,

For in every setback, there's wisdom to accost.

I once believed there was time to spare,

No need to rush, no need for care.

But time, relentless in its march, has shown

That every moment counts, every seed sown.

I ponder what could have been, what might have transpired,

But dwelling on the past leaves me mired.

Instead, I choose to focus on the road ahead,

To seize each moment, no matter where it's led.

For whom I am today is who I choose to be,

Defined not by the past, but by what I decree.

With courage in my heart and hope in my gaze,

I'll face the years ahead with steadfast praise.

So let the years stack up, let them come and go,

I'll greet each one with vigor, with a determined flow.

For in the end, it's not the years we've amassed,

But the legacy we leave, the memories that last.

CHAPTER 45
IN THE MIDDLE OF THE NIGHT

At 3 AM, the world's a silent frame,

A whisper loud, in stillness, it became.

A beam of light, through darkness, softly threads,

In search of dreams to fill the beds.

The wind, a melody outside the pane,

While birds are in trees, the moonlight entertains.

Within my ears, a ringing silence grows,

Seeking escape, from quiet, it flows.

My eyes traverse the darkness, lost and keen,

For remnants of a dream, once vivid, seen.

Comfort eludes the confines of my bed,

As unvoiced screams within my heart are shed.

No blame to cast, no reason to indict,

Like dripping taps that break the still of the night.

A sigh, my only tether to release,

Yearning for the solace of sweet peace.

In this nocturnal hour, I seek reprieve,

A moment's rest, in dreams, I long to weave.

Yet, in the quiet, my restless thoughts still leap,

All I desire is to return to quiet sleep.

CHAPTER 46
IN THE MIRROR'S GAZE

In the mirror's gaze, reflections dance,

Echoes of the soul, a fleeting trance.

It holds the truth, both stark and kind,

Revealing secrets of heart and mind.

In its depths, we see our faces,

Lines of time, our journey's embrace.

Each scar and dimple, every line,

A story told, a life defined.

It reflects our joys, our deepest pain,

Moments of loss and moments regained.

In its glassy depths, we find solace,

A silent witness to every promise.

Yet, on its surface, lies more than skin,

It shows the battles that lie within.

The struggle for love, for acceptance true,

Reflected back in shades of blue.

But in its gaze, we find the key,

To unlock the doors, to set us free.

For in the mirror, we see our worth,

A reminder that we're of infinite birth.

So let us gaze into its frame,

Embrace our flaws, without shame.

For in the mirror's silent stare,

We find the strength to truly care.

CHAPTER 47
IN THE QUIET STILLNESS

In the quiet stillness of contemplation's realm,

Amidst the fields of green, I am overwhelmed.

Reflections dance upon the stream of time,

As I ponder where I've been, and the mountain I climb.

Yesterday's whispers linger in the air,

Echoes of regrets and moments laid bare.

The words left unspoken, the truths untold,

In the tapestry of life, their threads unfold.

Years flow like a river, relentless and fast,

Leaving behind remnants of memories amassed.

In the mirror, wrinkles trace the passage of time,

Yet within, the spirit's flame continues to shine.

But amidst the somber shades of reminiscence,

A glimmer of light breaks through the dense.

A moment of clarity, a sudden epiphany,

Guiding me towards a newfound destiny.

I see the friendships forged in my youthful days,

And the love that blossomed in so many ways.

Though they may have faded, their essence remains,

Embedded in the heart's eternal chains.

As I gaze upon the horizon yet to unfold,

Life's journey reveals its secrets untold.

With each step forward, I embrace the unknown,

For in the middle of the rainbow, I have grown.

CHAPTER 48
IN THE REALM OF FORESIGHT

In the realm of foresight, yet still I tread,

My mind, a ceaseless guide, where wisdom is spread,

A relentless drumbeat to my conscious ear,

Urging caution, like a preacher sincere.

Guarding against the unexpected sway,

A pause to assess, to survey the fray,

Evaluating, preparing to defend,

Ensuring my stance will not bend.

Amidst the consensus of what has been,

Seeking resolutions, a path to glean,

In moments of pause, a blank stare,

Awaiting the courage to dare.

Exploring the attic of memories old,

Discovering treasures, stories untold,

With dedication akin to a quest,

Preparing for life's ultimate test.

CHAPTER 49
IN THE STILLNESS OF THE LATE NIGHT

In the stillness of the late night's hush,

I'm stirred awake by thoughts that rush.

Words dance in shadows, refusing to rest,

Demanding to be expressed, not suppressed.

They form a symphony, a silent plea,

Echoes of creativity longing to break free.

I toss and turn, seeking solace in sleep,

But the muse's whispers are too deep.

Like a relentless tide, they flood my mind,

Insisting I release them, to unwind.

Each syllable a spark, each phrase a flame,

Burning brightly in the night's domain.

So, I yield to the call of the restless muse,

Embracing the words it wants to infuse.

With pen in hand, I let them flow,

Capturing the magic of the late night's glow.

CHAPTER 50
IN THE TANGLE OF THE DAY

In the tangle of day, I am lost in dreams,

Grasping at visions, or so it seems,

Desires rise, a crescendo, they soar,

Tempting me to where I long to explore.

Prayer's escape, a natural plea,

For reality to match the dreams I see,

Navigating through ideas, ready to ignite,

Dreaming of abundance, refusing to take flight.

I know within, greatness awaits,

Just around the corner, beyond the gates,

This notion dispels any hint of gloom,

As I wait for the blessings yet to bloom.

I know, deep down, it's coming soon,

My wishes, my wants, like a sweet monsoon,

As clear as the sight of the full moon's light,

This certainty fuels my inner might.

CHAPTER 51
IN YOU

Like the sun at its zenith, fiercely bright,

You illumine each room with your light;

As a garden in full, resplendent bloom,

Your beauty dispels even the deepest gloom.

As the Milky Way scatters stars through the night,

You're the reason my existence feels right;

Like green leaves that canopy the forest's heart,

You envelop me, never to part.

Like the blooms that unfurl at dawn's first light,

For whom the morning birds take flight,

Your every step flows with purpose and grace,

In this dance of life, you're my steadfast place.

Like the ocean's wave, gentle yet sure,

Your charm captivates, and your allure,

As playful as a bunny, soft and small,

Intriguing and humorous, you enthralled.

My lucky charm, close and dear,

Without you, chaos would be near;

The wind that fills my sails and guides me,

At every pinnacle, it's you who resides.

My river's course, naturally flowing,

My library is vast, ever all-knowing,

The one my heart loves without cease,

In you, my life finds its peace.

CHAPTER 52
IN YOUR EMBRACE

In the night's soft, embracing hold,

Your touch, a story yet untold,

Draws you nearer, heart to heart,

In this quiet, we are never apart.

Your warmth breathes life into the air,

As we lie entwined without a care.

Your heartbeat's rhythm, close to mine,

In harmony, our souls align.

Your skin, a canvas smooth and fine,

Under fingertips, a divine sign.

Your soft murmurs, a gentle call,

Bringing peace to my soul's brawl.

"Is your love for me true?" you softly inquire,

Under the moon's gentle, silver fire.

And so, I whisper back, with love imbued,

"Yes, my dear, it's true, endlessly I do."

CHAPTER 53
INSPIRATION

In the heart of every soul resides a flame,

A flickering light that calls your name.

It whispers softly in the depths of night,

Guiding you through the darkness, shining bright.

When storms rage fierce and skies turn gray,

It's the beacon that leads you on your way.

With courage as your compass, you'll find,

The strength within leaves doubt behind.

For every challenge is a chance to grow,

To spread your wings and let your spirit flow.

Embrace each moment, both joy and pain,

For they are the threads in life's intricate chain.

Believe in yourself, in your dreams so grand,

For you hold the power in your own hand.

With passion as your fuel, you'll soar high,

And reach the stars that light up the sky.

So let your heart be your guiding star,

And let your dreams take flight, near and far.

With each step you take, you'll find your way,

And transform the darkest night into day.

CHAPTER 54
INTO THE DARK

Into a room of darkness deep I stride,

A void of nothingness on every side.

An endless bloom of emptiness unfurled,

No form or shape in this shadowed world.

A door that leads to naught but empty air,

As memories sought seem scarce and rare.

With a longing gaze, I search the void for clues,

Feeling for walls, for something to use.

Direction lost, the path ahead unclear,

What lies beyond, consumed by fear.

My hands move blindly, in the hope they grope,

For that which I seek, in shadows, I scope.

Then, in the dark, a form begins to take,

Under my touch, a chance I dare to make.

With pressure right, a switch beneath my thumb,

The darkness flees, and the light has come.

In that swift turn, fate unveils its face,

The room alight, gone is the dark's embrace.

A simple flick, and shadows are dispelled,

In the light's warm glow, my fears are quelled.

CHAPTER 55
IT'S RAINING OUT

It's raining out, deep in my thoughts again

In dream like state about now and then

Reflecting on the past I long for

Comparing to the present I adore

What was is now a memory, a story

What's now, sometimes is still a concern and worry

In overall I'm still moving through life

Although sometimes it feels like on the edge of a knife

And even though sometimes I feel the pressure

I still believe, within the normal measure

And so I pray before each knight

So that tomorrow will be great and bright

I do believe this and it does

All just works out with minimal fuss

As I remember all the past

All did work out rather fast

The clouds will part and the sun will shine

And all I wished for will be mine

I know this deep within my soul

I somehow always reached my goal

Why am I saying this out loud

Feels like I'm shouting it out

As long as we pray and believe it must

God will not break the sacred trust!

CHAPTER 56
KIEV RUS IN SHADOWS DEEP

In shadows deep, where legends dwell,

Rus sons and daughters rose and fell.

With hearts ablaze and spirits keen,

They carved their fates, in realms unseen.

Beneath the crescent moon's soft glow,

Across the vast, untamed snow,

The brave and bold, with eyes afire,

Kindled the flames of deep desire.

In whispers low, the forests speak

Of warriors strong and never weak.

With axes raised and shields so stout,

They faced their foes, in battle clout.

From Novgorod to the Black Sea's shore,

Their defiant roars through valleys bore.

Against the tide of time they stood,

For freedom's breath, for kin and blood.

Vladimir's baptism, a crossroad's turn,

Where pagan pyres no longer burn.

Yet, in their hearts, the old gods stayed,

With Perun's might, in secret prayed.

The Dnieper's rapids, fierce and wild,

Witnessed the spirit, unreconciled.

As Varangian boats dared to leap,

The river's gods, their watch did keep.

Yaroslav the Wise, with the law in hand,

United Rus', a vast expanse of land.

His wisdom sowed, for years to reap,

In golden words, his legacy is steep.

For every stone in Kiev's grand walls,

A tale of bravery, when duty calls.

The Rus', in history's deep weave,

A tapestry of dreams to believe.

So, hear the call, the brave, the defiant,

In every heart, a warrior giant.

Across the ages, their echoes ring,

In Slavic souls, forever sing.

CHAPTER 57
KNIGHT OF VALOR

In lands consumed by dread and fright,

There lived a knight of truest might.

His heart ablaze with valor's flame,

He pledged to shield the meek, the same.

For justice, truth, and those defenseless,

He rode forth, unwavering and relentless.

To guard the farms, the humble hearth,

He swore to shield them from all dearth.

Against the wicker's darkened guise,

He stood firm, beneath the skies.

A beacon of virtue, strong and fair,

To the downtrodden, he was ever there.

So, heed, all ye who harbor ill intent,

For his watchful gaze is never spent.

No hand shall rise to cause distress,

While under his protective caress.

God's hand shall guide, no foe shall creep,

As champions like him their vigil keep.

In tales of old, this truth we seek,

That the strong are tasked to defend the weak!

CHAPTER 58
LIFE, A WINDING ROAD

Life, a winding road upon the sea,

Balancing on waves of chance, yet free,

Fear's tempestuous waves, rock the way,

While love's gentle tide guides night and day.

Opportunity, a beacon shining bright,

Inspiration's breeze, a wondrous flight,

Belief, the compass leading through the night,

Life's journey, a dance within the light.

Each wave, a trial, a test to face,

Yet in their ebb and flow, we find our grace,

For on this sea of circumstance, we sail,

Navigating through storms, without fail.

Though waves may toss and turn us to and from,

In the end, it's our spirit that will grow,

For life is but a voyage, wild and grand,

Balancing on waves, we find our land.

CHAPTER 59
LIFE'S VAST TAPESTRY

In life's vast tapestry, threads may tangle,

And paths may twist, leaving us to wrangle.

The journey is long, oft seems unfair,

A labyrinth of trials laid bare.

The road we tread, with twists and turns,

Ignites our fears, as anxiety churns.

Like a sinister harp, our nerves it plays,

Casting shadows over the brightest days.

Entwined in thoughts, beyond our reign,

Some moments drenched in ceaseless pain.

Yet, when we rise from despair's deep cup,

We find ourselves, still, somewhat stuck.

Let not the minutiae cloud your sight,

Focus on dreams, and in their delight.

Fix your gaze upon the desires' sphere,

And whisper your wants into the universe's ear.

Eyes on the prize, let nothing stall,

With steadfast aim, you'll conquer all.

The goal ahead, though far it seems,

Is closer than in your wildest dreams.

For life's a journey, not a race,

And every challenge we must face.

With hope as our compass, and dreams as our guide,

Towards our destiny, we'll stride.

CHAPTER 60
LIKE RAINDROPS, JOURNEY OF THE SOUL

I am sitting here dwelling on a thought that may not be my own

Wrapped up in a depth of wondering why

How at our life's beginning, at its dawn

Souls fall like pure raindrops from a cloud in the sky

To walk our path, to push to pound

Step by step, each in our unique sway

Like a raindrop running along the ground

Gathering whatever it touches along the way

Is our life's really ours to will

Is the free will just a reality screen

Do we really have choices or is it still

That we just follow what was predetermined and foreseen

Do we live an illusion or what

Our perception is really only at arm's length

Each one is like a raindrop; we all have our spot

And within this spot is our only choices, weakness and strength

We fall upon this reality in our physical form

To experience and gather any knowledge

Going through sunshine and various storm

To gain what you won't learn in college

This physical sensor of what we are

To gather and what we call, live through

Our soul is dropped here for this from afar

And this I believe in my heart to be true

And when we are tired of gathering experiences and stuff

After we are through running our life course

When our bodies are saying enough is enough

Like raindrops we evaporate back to the source

Sitting here looking around my personal spot

Voices inside my head whispering in fear

I wonder about this question a lot

What is our true purpose and why are we really here?

CHAPTER 61
LOVE TORNADO

Love is not a simple notion

A title wave of the emotions

Like mountain stream out of the ground

Can quench your thirst after you drowned

Can put you on the mountaintop

Or push you off and let you drop

Can cushion from the highest fall

Or dig under you still a deeper hole

Can make you think that you can fly

Or make you feel you want to die

Can turn your frown upside down

Or stand and smile while you drown

Can bring down any blocking wall

Or build them high so you feel small

Can clear the clouds in the sky

Or make you don't want to open your eyes

You try to think that you're in charge

Then realize that's false in large

Thinking you can control your feelings

Is like trying to sleep on the ceilings

Seems like a very tiny sway

Can make the rainbow become gray

Why can someone feel so good

Next moment can become like wood

There has to be a reason why

We bounce from love to want to cry

Why can the love that we feel

Stay in the solid state for real

I want feelings of joy and infatuation

To conquer every situation

Hold on to great things at the seem

And love for all will be supreme

CHAPTER 62
MIND'S STAGE

In the shadows of my mind's stage,

Unwanted feelings start to engage,

A new emotion, yet old and worn,

Resurfaces as if reborn.

Familiar scenes, familiar faces,

Echoes of past, familiar places,

A recurring play, a scripted show,

But the outcome, I already know.

I've trod these paths, I've felt these pains,

I've danced in circles, I've played these games,

Yet here they are, the same old thoughts,

Creeping in when I least sought.

But I refuse to be ensnared,

By the ghosts of what I've dared,

I'll close the curtains, end the play,

And walk from this stage, without delay.

For I've seen this show once before,

And I won't let it haunt me anymore,

I'll cast aside these shadows, bitter and sore,

And embrace the light, forevermore.

CHAPTER 63
MISERY LOVES COMPANY

In times of anger and despair

When all seems hopeless and lost

When life seems more than you can bear

Depression peaking at its most

When happy thoughts seem far away

When your whole world is crashing down

When hard to see a better way

And all there is a heavy frown

It seems that there's no place to hide

No one can bring you into light

It's hard to see another side

A wall is all that's in your sight

No apatite to enjoy food

When alcohol is only call

Looking around you see no good

And all you feel is a fall

You yell and scream at all who's there

It is my friend so plain to see

As much as it is so unfair

That misery loves company

CHAPTER 64
IN THE DEPTHS OF YOUR HEART

In the depths of your heart, a spark ignites,

A flame of courage, burning bright.

Through trials and tribulations, you rise,

With determination in your eyes.

Though storms may rage, and winds may blow,

You stand firm, ready to grow.

For within you lie a strength untold,

A resilience that never grows old.

With each step forward, you blaze a trail,

Breaking barriers, without fail.

You turn setbacks into steppingstones,

And face challenges with a heart of stone.

So, keep shining, like the stars above,

With unwavering faith and boundless love.

For in your journey, you inspire,

A testament to the human desire.

CHAPTER 65
WHEN LIFE'S ROAD SEEMS LONG

When life's road seems long and steep,

And challenges make you want to weep,

Remember the strength within your soul,

And let determination take control.

With every setback, every fall,

Rise again, stand tall.

For within you burns a fire,

A burning desire that won't expire.

Embrace the journey, every twist and turn,

For with each lesson, you'll grow and learn.

Believe in yourself, and you will find,

The power to leave your doubts behind.

You have the courage to face your fears,

To overcome obstacles and dry your tears.

With perseverance as your guiding light,

You'll conquer mountains, and reach new heights.

So, keep moving forward, one step at a time,

With faith in your heart and purpose in mind.

For you are capable of greatness, it's true,

Believe in yourself, and the world will too.

CHAPTER 66
MY LIVING JOY

In every breath, my living joy resides,

A flame that within my spirit abides.

It dances bright in each day's light,

Filling my heart with pure delight.

In laughter shared with those I hold dear,

In moments of peace that draw me near, I

n simple pleasures, both big and small,

My living joy embraces all.

It blooms in the beauty of nature's grace,

In the warmth of a familiar embrace,

In the melody of a favorite song,

My living joy is forever strong.

Through life's ups and downs, it remains,

A steadfast beacon through joy and pains.

For in each moment, I find it anew,

My living joy, is forever true.

CHAPTER 67
MY YEARS

My years are stacked on a closet shelf

Holding on tight to all they gained

And l, the former bases of myself

Walking ahead with what I gained

The youth I knew and wasted away

Is but an analogy for the remaining

I smirked at life's presented tray

Trying to avoid all types of framing

Thinking, there's plenty of time still left

No need to rush anything yet

But time in its persistent theft

Left me with wondering instead

To wonder what I could have been

What I could learn and then create

Or where and what I could have seen

And how it would adjust my fate

I guess I know who I am

No point for regret or sorrow

Face passing years without a slam

With full attention on a brighter tomorrow!

CHAPTER 68
NIGHT SWEATS

Like a storm that rages at sea, my thoughts pound,

Creating chaos, where silence once found.

In the night's quiet, like a battlefield spent,

My mind wearies from the tumult it's meant.

My body, an ice floe adrift in the dark,

Head drenched as if caught in the rain's harsh mark.

My pillow, a sponge, soaked with the sweat of dread,

In the hush of night, my fears are fed.

Turning and twisting, like a leaf in the wind,

Seeking solace where none is pinned.

I pray like a sailor in a storm's fierce clutch,

Longing for peace that eludes my touch.

Rolling quietly, like fog over land,

Comfort was elusive, not as I had planned.

Thus, I wish and fish in the depths of night,

For a dawn of calm, for an end to my plight.

CHAPTER 69
NO CONTROL

In the grasp of illusions, control we seek,

A mere shadow's game, both strong and weak.

To reign every tide, command every wave,

Is a fanciful dance with the time we crave.

Lofty as dreams, yet bound by the earth,

Like petals that shroud the sunflower's girth.

Emotions crescendo, then spill and cascade,

Rippling through doubts, perpetually swayed.

In the mirage of truth and fable's allure,

The ego persistently taps, ever so sure.

Stress patterns down like relentless rain,

Clouds of bewilderment, a numbing refrain.

Paralyzed yet racing, a paradoxical feat,

In the silent uproar, an admission of defeat.

Yet within this turmoil, a whisper entices,

Toward the gentle truce that compromises voices.

CHAPTER 70
POETIC SEEN

In the twilight's embrace, where day and night entwine,

There lies a meadow, kissed by the sun's last shine.

A canvas painted in hues of lavender and gold,

Where whispered secrets of nature unfold.

Here, the grass sways gently to a silent melody,

As if each blade were a poet in harmony.

The air is filled with the scent of wildflowers,

Their fragrance weaving dreams in twilight hours.

In the distance, a solitary oak stands tall,

Its branches reaching skyward, embracing all.

Its leaves rustle softly in the evening breeze,

A symphony of nature, swaying with ease.

Above, the sky is a tapestry of stars,

Twinkling diamonds scattered from afar.

The moon, a silent sentinel, watches overall,

Casting its silver glow like a celestial ball.

Amidst this poetic scene, time seems to slow,

As if nature itself were putting on a show.

Here, in this tranquil haven, all is at peace,

A moment of beauty that will never cease.

CHAPTER 71
POETIC SYMPHONY

In this hall where echoes dwell,

A poetic symphony begins to swell.

Each word a note, each line a chord,

Crafting beauty, stroke by stroke, word by word.

The rustling of the crowd grows still,

As verses rise and hearts they fill.

The imagery, like music, flows,

In cadences only the heart knows.

A metaphor, a flute's soft trill,

Similes, the strings that thrill.

Alliteration, drums in sync,

Personification makes us think.

The stanza breaks, a pause, a rest,

Building suspense within the chest.

Then on it rushes, wild and free,

A crescendo of pure imagery.

Each poet, a musician skilled,

With words and rhythms, the air is filled.

The maestro waves, the verses fly,

A tapestry is woven underneath the mind's sky.

And as the final lines are read,

Applause echoes, wide and spread.

The curtain falls, but still it stays,

The memory of poetic plays.

In every heart, the music lingers,

Crafted by invisible fingers.

For poetry, in essence, true,

Plays forever, for me, for you.

9 798889 383513 7